HOW TO BE

MINDFUL

ANNA BARNES

An Hachette UK Company
www.hachette.co.uk

Vie Books, an imprint of Summersdale Publishers Ltd
Part of Octopus Publishing Group Limited
Carmelite House
50 Victoria Embankment
LONDON
EC4Y 0DZ
UK

www.summersdale.com

Printed and bound in India

ISBN: 978-1-78685-199-4

Substantial discounts on bulk quantities of Summersdale books are available to corporations, professional associations and other organisations. For details contact general enquiries: telephone: +44 (0) 1243 771107 or email: enquiries@summersdale.com.

CONTENTS

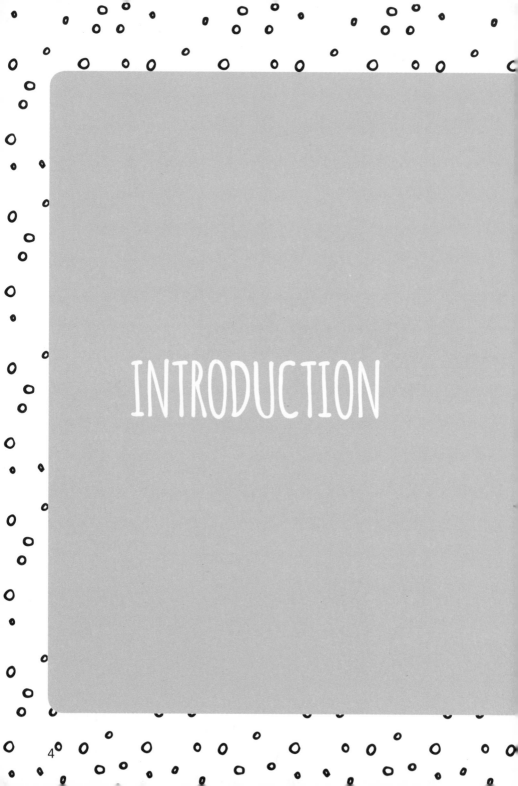

INTRODUCTION

Mindfulness is about focusing on the magic of the present moment. Rather than fretting about the past or worrying about the future, the aim is to experience life as it unfolds moment by moment. This simple practice is immensely powerful. As we rush through our lives, mindfulness encourages us to stop constantly striving for something new or better and to embrace acceptance and gratitude. This allows us to tap into the joy and wonder in our lives, and to listen to the wisdom of our hearts. This book will show you how to experience small but beautiful moments of mindfulness every day and so guide you along the path to finding more peace and contentment in your life.

A LITTLE BIT
OF MINDFULNESS
EVERY DAY

A NEW DAY BEGINS.

A REFRESHING WAY TO START THE DAY

On waking in the morning, rather than springing out of bed to start your busy day, spend a few moments becoming aware of your surroundings. Listen to the sounds around you and notice what thoughts are in your mind. Sit up straight, place your feet on the floor, and tune in to your body. Focus on your breathing and allow your stomach to rise and fall. Imagine that you are breathing in the morning light. Visualise each breath flooding your body with golden light from the rising sun. Feel energised, ready for the day ahead.

What a benediction
is this fragrance of
the early morning!

Sarah Smiley

LET YOUR STRESSES FLOAT AWAY

Visualisation can be a powerful meditation tool. If you are feeling anxious, visualise a hot air balloon and imagine that you are putting all your stress and negativity into the balloon. Then watch it gently float away into the distance, taking your worries and concerns with it.

START SMALL

Mindfulness is not something you achieve overnight; it is a habit which is developed gradually over time. The best approach is to take baby steps. Start by picking one or two opportunities to treat with a mindful attitude every day. You might decide to be mindful every time you brush your teeth, walk to the car, open a door or make a cup of tea, for example. Whichever action you choose, make sure you give your whole attention to it. When you open a door, watch your hand grasp the doorknob, feel the weight of the door as you pull it open, and hear the sounds of whatever is on the other side of the doorway... If you do this every time you open a door, you will be amazed at how automatic this process becomes. This simple ritual will allow mindfulness to establish a foothold in your life. All you need to do is take baby steps and commit to being mindful for a few seconds several times a day.

LEARN THE RIGHT TECHNIQUE

You can learn mindfulness in numerous ways to suit your preferences and budget. If you're an auditory learner, you could buy a mindfulness CD or podcast to guide you into a meditative state. If you prefer to learn directly from a teacher, consider signing up to a local introductory class or investing in some one-to-one tuition. Many yoga courses and retreats also include mindfulness meditation as part of the curriculum. Learning in a group has the benefit of a strong atmosphere of community and friendship, but if you prefer to learn in the privacy of your own home, try taking an online course such as the one at www.bemindful.co.uk.

INSTRUCTION FOR LIFE:

PAY ATTENTION.

Whatever the present
moment contains, accept it
as if you had chosen it.

Eckhart Tolle

USE VISUAL CUES

Being mindful is not difficult to do – it's the remembering that's the key! Place inspiring pictures and notes around your home to remind you and your family to 'be mindful', 'pause' and 'take a breath'. These visual triggers can be all you need to snap you back to the present moment.

I CAN
&
I WILL

THINGS
TO BE
GRATEFUL
FOR

Start a daily gratitude journal. List all the positive things in your life – from the small things that make you smile, such as the view from your window, to the bigger things, such as your health or your family. At night, list three things you were grateful for during the day and you'll soon start focusing naturally on the positives.

EVERYDAY MINDFULNESS

Many of us go through our daily routines on automatic pilot, barely noticing what we are doing. An easy way to focus your attention on the present moment is to focus on simple tasks. For instance, make your bed with 100 per cent focus and attention each morning so you create a calm transition from bedroom and sleep to the outside world and the rest of your day. Similarly, when cleaning your teeth or brushing your hair, notice every sensory detail. You might also find it useful to sit quietly for a few minutes in the morning so that you can calmly contemplate the day ahead, instead of rushing straight into your day's activities.

DIGITAL DETOX

The non-stop stream of information we receive from mobiles, computers and TVs can be overwhelming. It's a good idea to give our mental 'inbox' a break from time to time. Turn off your devices, hide all gadgets and give yourself some time off from the endless technological invasion in your life.

The greatest step towards a life of simplicity is to learn to let go.

Steve Maraboli

SEE THE GOOD EVERYWHERE.

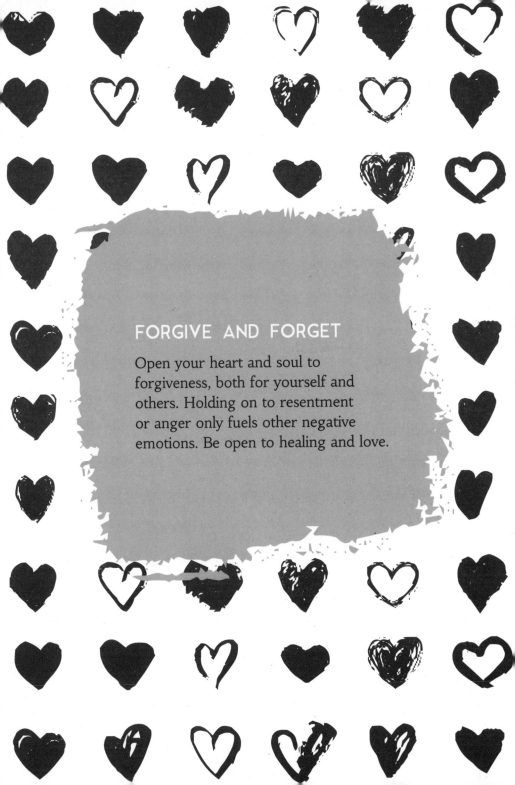

FORGIVE AND FORGET

Open your heart and soul to
forgiveness, both for yourself and
others. Holding on to resentment
or anger only fuels other negative
emotions. Be open to healing and love.

CALM READING

Notice today how you scan over most of your reading material. Slow down and read with your full attention, absorbing the full meaning of the words and not skipping sections. How different does this feel from usual? Does it make you feel more relaxed? Do the words affect you more deeply?

Happiness is a Journey, not a Destination.

BREATHE INTO TENSION

If you encounter a difficult
situation today, notice which
parts of your body feel tense,
then breathe into the area to help
you relax. Remind yourself that
challenging moments always pass.

The greatest weapon against
stress is our ability to choose
one thought over another.

William James

THE

ORDI

NARY

CAN BE

EXTRAORDINARY

Mindfulness
is seeing
things with
fresh eyes.

ORDINARY INTO EXTRAORDINARY

Take a daily routine activity, such as cleaning your teeth, and be curious and alert about yourself, noticing every sensory detail. Pay attention to the contours of your mouth and the sensation of the brush against each tooth. Notice if you're thinking ahead to what you're doing next and if so, gently bring your attention back to the present.

STAND FIRM, LIKE A TREE

A great way to ground yourself
when you're in the midst of turmoil,
is to take some deep breaths and
visualise roots growing from your
feet into the ground. Stand firm
like a tree, while the chaos around
you blows through your branches
and disappears on the breeze.

In the midst of movement and chaos, keep stillness inside of you.

Deepak Chopra

The most important thing
about being mindful

is remembering to be mindful!

MAKE MORE MEMORIES

Don't take things for granted. Everyday moments, when experienced fully, can become lifelong memories – from savouring the first freshly picked strawberries of the season or the blackbird's song outside your window to holding a new-born child.

ARRIVE MINDFULLY

Whenever you arrive somewhere, give yourself a moment to 'check in'. Become aware of how your body is feeling – especially any aches and tensions. Take note of what emotions you are carrying. Acknowledge all of this, taking no more than a minute, and you will be centred and present, ready to move on.

An awake heart is like a sky that pours light.

Hāfez

MAKE
TODAY
A
'NO RUSH'
DAY.

STAY GROUNDED

When you're in a rush – dashing
around the supermarket or taking
the dog for a quick walk – bring
your awareness to your feet.
Slow down slightly and feel your
feet connect you to the ground.
This will help you to gain a sense
of equilibrium and balance.

DON'T JUMP TO CONCLUSIONS

There is great truth in the familiar saying, 'Don't judge a book by its cover.' We often prejudge people by their appearance or the sound of their voice. Being mindful means seeing everything in the present moment, without leaping to unfounded conclusions.

PAUSE

IT'S WHAT GIVES YOU YOUR POWER.

YOU ALWAYS HAVE A CHOICE
IN HOW TO RESPOND.

CHOOSE YOUR REACTION

Strong emotions, such as anger, hurt or fear, can erupt very quickly. But there's usually a split second in which you can pause before you react. When you feel something inside you being triggered, become mindful of your breath. Notice the sensations in your body. Realise you have a choice about what you do next before you react.

PRACTISE MINDFUL LISTENING

We often find that when we listen to others
we are concentrating on what to say next,
filling up our minds with our own opinions
or even speaking out of turn. Try listening
with mindfulness – hear the person without
judgement or the need to immediately
express a view. Be aware that the word 'listen'
can be shuffled around to spell 'silent'.

BREATHE INTO YOUR BELLY

Take a moment to 'belly breathe' for a greater flow of oxygen and instant calm. Breathe in deeply, allowing your stomach to rise outwards. On the out-breath, allow your stomach to fall back.

LET GO OF THE

STRESS OF PERFECTIONISM.

CONNECT WITH PEOPLE

Take time out to sit on a bench or a window seat
in a cafe and watch people go by. Don't read,
talk or catch up on social media – just people-
watch. Feel connected to everyone and watch
them with an open mind and compassion.

The more we notice
things to appreciate,
the more they
seem to grow.

STICK WITH IT

Developing a daily mindfulness practice takes patience and determination. It can be hard work to keep pulling your mind back to the present moment. There will be challenges and obstacles to overcome, not least the fact that the benefits of mindfulness may be quite subtle at first. There may be times when you want to throw in the towel, but be determined. If you persevere, you will learn from obstacles and overcome them. Your ability will improve and the benefits will start to become more obvious. You will start to feel more present, peaceful and alive. Whenever you feel your patience wavering, remind yourself that mindfulness works like a muscle – the more you exercise it, the stronger it gets.

THE POWER OF THE MIND

The mind… can be compared
to the sky, covered by
layers of cloud which
hide its true nature.

Kalu Rinpoche

YOU ARE NOT
YOUR THOUGHTS

Do your thoughts overwhelm and confuse you?
Do you wish your mind had an 'off' button?
Much of our suffering stems from the fact
that we think our thoughts are the core of our
being. We identify with our thoughts and allow
them to dictate how we feel. As our thoughts
are often 'noisy', negative and chaotic, it's no
wonder we struggle. The solution lies not in
trying to get rid of our thoughts altogether but
in stopping our habit of identifying with them.
Simply observe your thoughts without judgement
and let them go. You do not have to be a slave
to your thoughts and feelings. What gives
them fuel and makes them real is the attention
you bring to them. Take away that attention,
and that thought or feeling ceases to exist!

NOTICE WHAT
DISTRACTS YOU

We each have unique tendencies or thoughts
that pull us away from the present moment.
Start paying attention to your thoughts
and jot down the types of thoughts that
distract you most often. Do you have a
tendency to dwell on the past or the future?
Are you consumed with thoughts of guilt,
fear, regret or worry? Do you ruminate
on achieving perfection or success, wealth
and recognition? Writing these tendencies
down can help you become more mindful
about what is going on in your head when
you stray from the present moment. This
insight can lead you to mindfulness.

LISTEN TO YOUR HEART AND TRUST YOUR INSTINCTS.

STOP ASSUMING
THE WORST

If your mind is racing and you are consumed with worry, are you scaring yourself with 'what-ifs'? What-ifs and imagined scenarios may seem incredibly real but they are a figment of our imagination. A large proportion of the things we imagine never actually happen. Let's say you take your cat to the vets because he has stopped eating and you spend the day before the appointment worrying that the vet will discover a terrible disease. In reality, the vet finds a splinter in your cat's gum and removes it, solving the problem. Yet you spent the previous day gripped with anxiety. If worrying is controlling your life, it's time to take control. The second you realise you are dwelling on a worst-case scenario, bring yourself back to the present. Remind yourself that you are not a fortune teller! Worrying serves no purpose other than to make you feel anxious. Focus on the facts of a situation and on what is (rather than what-ifs!).

Accept people for
who they are,

including yourself!

FORGIVE YOURSELF

Self-compassion is essential when learning mindfulness. You will not be able to sustain mindfulness 100 per cent of the time. You may be 'too busy' to practise or forget to practise altogether. You may be unable to stop your mind from wandering, or you may find yourself thinking about being mindful rather than practising being mindful! The ability to forgive yourself at these times is crucial. Self-compassion will enable you to pick yourself up, dust yourself off and try again. If you beat yourself up every time you falter, you will be far less likely to stick to the kind of regular practice which will impact on your health and happiness.

THERE IS NO DESTINATION!

When we embark on a new project, we normally have a goal or destination in mind. The beauty of mindfulness is that it is a process; there is no end destination. You cannot exist outside of the present moment. Life is what is happening to you right now. So the only goal when practising mindfulness is to be fully present. It can be helpful to remind yourself of this on a regular basis. You might like to write the following mantra on a piece of paper and put it somewhere where you can see it every day: There is nowhere more important for you to be than right here, right now.

WAYS TO INVITE
MINDFULNESS
INTO YOUR LIFE

GIVE IN TO YOUR CREATIVE URGE

Try something creative –
draw or paint a picture,
write a story about your
childhood or play a piece of
music. Don't worry about
the quality of what you're
producing, and don't hold
back – the most important
thing is to immerse yourself
in the joy of creating!

Listening to music can be a great mindfulness exercise. Choose music that is soothing: instrumental or classical are good choices. Begin by sitting with a comfortable, upright posture. Choose a space where you can minimise any outer distractions and be sure to turn off your phone, computer and television. Spend a few moments breathing fully and completely, immersing yourself in your inhalation and exhalation. As you begin to listen to the music, focus on the sound and vibration of each note. Notice any feelings that the music conjures up for you and any sensations that occur in your body as you listen. If other thoughts creep into your head, gently bring your attention back to the music. Afterwards, notice how much calmer you feel.

STOP THE CLOCK!

Plan a mindful weekend without clocks or watches. Listen to your body instead – you choose when to get up, when to eat, what tasks you feel like doing and the length of time you spend on them.

We have only now, only
this single eternal moment
opening and unfolding
before us, day and night.

Jack Kornfield

SAVOUR HOUSEWORK

Here's a great way to turn housework from a chore into an enjoyable activity: be completely present as you wash, scrub, dust and hoover – and do it without rushing. Savour every sensory detail. While washing up for example, notice every rainbow bubble, the warm water and the shining dishes. Feel a sense of satisfaction at a small job well done.

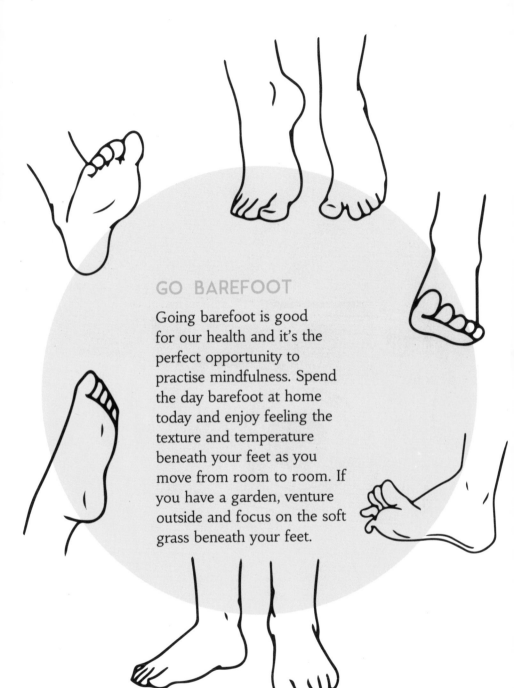

GO BAREFOOT

Going barefoot is good for our health and it's the perfect opportunity to practise mindfulness. Spend the day barefoot at home today and enjoy feeling the texture and temperature beneath your feet as you move from room to room. If you have a garden, venture outside and focus on the soft grass beneath your feet.

BE AWAKE TO NEW EXPERIENCES

When travelling to a new place, it is easy
to get distracted by taking photographs
and buying souvenirs. Make sure you get
the most out of the experience by bringing
your presence and full attention to all
that you experience. Savour the sights,
sounds and smells of your new location.

LOOK FOR THINGS TO BE THANKFUL FOR.

TRY SOMETHING NEW

You are instinctively being mindful whenever your brain is engaged in something unfamiliar. So make it your goal to try new things from time to time, whether that's learning a musical instrument or going to an art class. If you feel anxiety, fear or resistance when facing a new activity, mindfully notice that you are experiencing fear of the unknown. Be kind to yourself. Instead of shutting down or holding back, simply switch to an activity you find less scary to begin with. Whether it's skydiving or a salsa class, by slowly building confidence you can enjoy new hobbies and experience more moments of mindfulness.

Put your ear down close to
your soul and listen hard.

Anne Sexton

PAUSE BEFORE ANSWERING THE PHONE

Allow the telephone to ring three times before you reply, so that you can become aware of your breath and speak from a centred and calm space.

TAKE ADVANTAGE OF QUEUES

Turn inconvenient moments in your
day into opportunities for mindfulness.
If you're stuck in a queue at the
supermarket or in a traffic jam, become
aware of how your body, posture and
thoughts are affected by the situation.

Life happens.

Let it be.

TAKE A
POWER SHOWER

Transform your shower or bath
by bringing your full attention
to the experience. Feel the warm
water against your skin and listen
to the sound it makes. Savour the
scent of the soap and shampoo
and be aware of the variety of
textures beneath your hands.
Imagine that you are washing
yourself clean of any negativity.

GET DRESSED MINDFULLY

As you get dressed and undressed, slow the process down and observe whether your movements are comfortable and flowing, or hasty and rushed. Notice the textures and fabrics of your clothes and how they feel on your skin. Value the fact that you are able to make the decision over what you wear today.

CONQUER INFORMATION OVERLOAD

Reduce your information consumption. Cancel subscriptions for magazines you barely have time to read and unsubscribe from catalogues, junk mail and emails. A cluttered mind is a stressed mind. Free up your mind and make space for the whispers of your heart and soul.

A MINDFUL
BODY

TUNE IN TO
YOUR BODY

The next time you seek out a sugary snack, stop and think about how you are feeling. People often turn to food in an attempt to self-soothe or deal with stressful situations. Recognise that you are looking for something to eat that you think will bring you satisfaction. Sit down and be fully present with this craving. Awareness can often lessen the desire. Maybe you don't need that chocolate biscuit after all!

DO A 'BODY SWEEP'

Research shows that our emotions manifest in our body. For example, negative emotions often cause people to tense the muscles in their jaw and around their eyes and mouth. With repeated stress, these muscles can become sore and tight. One of the key ways to balance your mind–body connection is to stop and give yourself a 'body sweep'.

Sit quietly and systematically scan your body, starting at the top of your head and moving down over your face, the back of your head, your shoulders, arms, hands, torso, hips, legs and feet. As you do this, notice the sensations you feel. Are there any areas of tension, pressure or discomfort? If so, breathe into these areas and allow them to soften and relax. Practising this body sweep on a regular basis can help you become more alert to the messages of your body. The tension you discover might be a 'gut feeling' about a choice you're making or a headache may indicate that you need to pay attention to a health issue. By exploring the link between your body and mind, you will start to notice which parts of the body are stimulated or shut down when you experience a particular emotion. 'Softening' these areas can help release the tension or emotion stored there.

ARE YOU SITTING MINDFULLY?

Bring your awareness to your
chair or the ground and become
aware of pressures against your
body and textures on your skin.
Shift your weight to give you
greater comfort and notice
any areas of tension such as
shoulders, lower back or neck.

EVERYTHING HAPPENS FOR A REASON.

BREATHE IN CALM

Wherever you are, you can incorporate a calm, breathing meditation into your day. Start by becoming aware of your breath as it enters and leaves your nostrils. Breathe to your own rhythm. After a few breaths, focus on breathing in and breathing out the feelings you wish to nurture:

I BREATHE IN CALM. I BREATHE OUT CALM.
I BREATHE IN PEACE. I BREATHE OUT PEACE.
I BREATHE IN LOVE. I BREATHE OUT LOVE.
I BREATHE IN STRENGTH. I BREATHE OUT STRENGTH.
I BREATHE IN HARMONY. I BREATHE OUT HARMONY.

Create as many lines to your meditation as you wish, using words that are meaningful to you and the situation you find yourself in. This meditation is especially helpful if you're about to do something you feel nervous about: a job interview, a meeting with your child's teacher or any other important task.

MINDFUL MOVEMENT

Mindful exercise is about performing physical activity while focusing inward. This allows you to get more in touch with your body. The idea is to let go of distractions and unrelated thoughts, and focus your attention on your breath, movements and sensations. If you do this whilst working out, you will enhance your enjoyment, decrease your chances of injury, and even improve the efficacy of the exercise you're doing. Most importantly, it will help you develop a healthy and loving relationship with your body. Remember, you're aiming for quality, not quantity. Try turning off your TV or iPod and bringing your attention to your breath and your movements while you are jogging, cycling, swimming or lifting weights.

BY BEING
HAPPY IN THIS
MOMENT

YOU ARE
CREATING MORE
HAPPINESS.

GETTING FROM A TO B

As you walk from one place to another, become aware of your posture. Notice if you are rushing ahead, with your shoulders hunched with tension. Straighten your spine and lift your chest and be aware of your connection to the ground as each foot is placed in front of the other. Enjoy being alert and mindful while you walk. Throughout your day, take every opportunity to walk with peace and serenity – when walking to your car, moving from room to room at home or at work, or while out shopping, bring your full presence to the process of walking and you will glide serenely through your day.

You are
exactly
where

you need
to be.

MINDFUL EATING

If you regularly wolf down your food without really tasting it, start practising mindfulness whenever you eat. As you prepare your food, savour every culinary aroma. When you sit down to eat, take a moment to quietly give thanks for the food in front of you. As you eat your meal, focus all your attention on the tastes, sounds, smells and sensations you are experiencing, rather than anything else going on around you. See if turning the TV or radio off and eating in silence makes you appreciate the food and the feeling of being full more than usual. Try placing your fork down in-between mouthfuls and chewing each mouthful slowly in order to relish every taste sensation.

LIKE CLOUDS
IN THE SKY,

EVERYTHING
IS IN A
CONSTANT
PROCESS OF
CHANGE.

SPIRITUAL
MINDFULNESS

Meditation practice
isn't about trying
to throw ourselves
away or become
something better. It's
about befriending
who we are already.

Pema Chödrön

SMILE THROUGHOUT YOUR BODY

If you are feeling a little low, try this healing smile meditation. Bring to mind someone or something that makes you smile or laugh – your best friend, your pet or your partner, for example. Soak in the warm feeling you get when you think about them and let the corners of your mouth curl up into a gentle smile. Let this smile gather joy and energy and breathe these good feelings into your heart. On each out-breath, direct this warm, happy glow around your body. Let it travel to all your organs – your lungs, heart, liver, kidneys and digestive system. Smile into each of them. Smile, and let this loving energy travel along your limbs – along your arms, hands, legs and feet. Keep visualising what makes you feel happy. Breathe it into your heart and keep radiating this happiness out around your body. Practise this healing smile meditation any time you are going through a rough patch or are having a bad day.

It's good to have an
end in mind, but in
the end what counts
is how you travel.

Orna Ross

AFFIRM IT, BELIEVE IT

Affirmations are quiet reminders that
you repeat to yourself, either during
your meditation or as you go about
your day. They can be particularly
helpful if you find you are stuck in
a negative thought loop. Choose an
affirmation that has meaning for you,
such as, 'Everything that is happening
now is happening for my ultimate good'
or 'I am at peace with the world'.

MEDITATE TO SWITCH OFF STRESS

The more frequently you worry, the more your sympathetic nervous system kicks in. This triggers your 'fight or flight' response – stress hormones are released into the bloodstream, heart rate increases, muscles contract and blood pressure rises. To reduce this stress response, you can consciously turn on the parasympathetic nervous system, which restores your body to a state of calm.

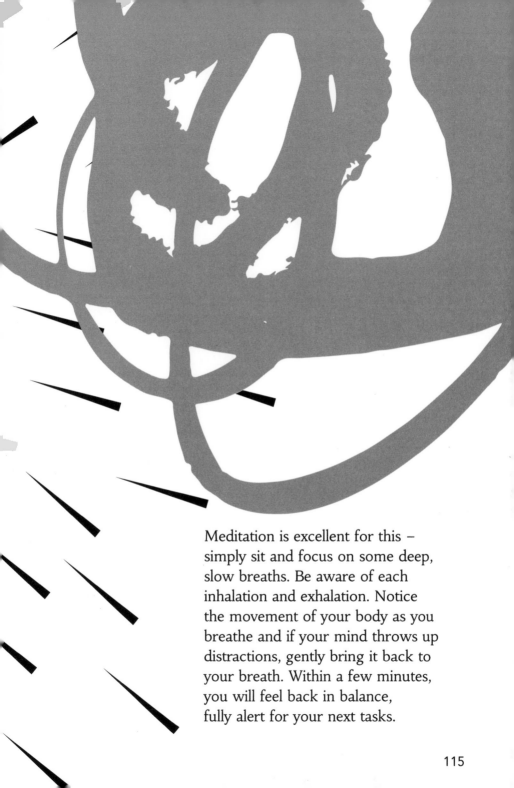

Meditation is excellent for this –
simply sit and focus on some deep,
slow breaths. Be aware of each
inhalation and exhalation. Notice
the movement of your body as you
breathe and if your mind throws up
distractions, gently bring it back to
your breath. Within a few minutes,
you will feel back in balance,
fully alert for your next tasks.

LET THOUGHTS COME AND GO

Many people think that the goal of
meditation is to achieve a blank mind,
with no thoughts at all, but having
thoughts while you meditate is perfectly
normal. In fact, it's what's supposed
to happen! Dealing with thoughts is
how mindfulness meditation works.
When you notice that you are distracted
by your thoughts, gently bring your
attention back to the object of your
meditation. Over time, this simple
practice will change how you relate
to distractions, and increase your
ability to focus and concentrate.

The time to be
happy is now,
The place to be
happy is here.

Robert G. Ingersoll

MAGICAL MANDALAS

Mandalas are geometric designs with a circular pattern that are used for meditation, prayer and healing. They have been used for thousands of years in the Buddhist and Hindu traditions as meditational tools to clear the mind. They have also been used in many therapeutic environments to help people unearth feelings that need to be expressed. Mandalas can be used in several ways. Creating your own mandala can facilitate your personal growth; helping you become more conscious of your inner thoughts and allowing you to tap into your creativity, without the need for any artistic expertise. You can also use mandalas to enhance your meditation practice. Choose a design that appeals to you and let your mind be absorbed by the patterns and colours you see. This soothes the busy, chattering mind and allows the creative mind to break free.

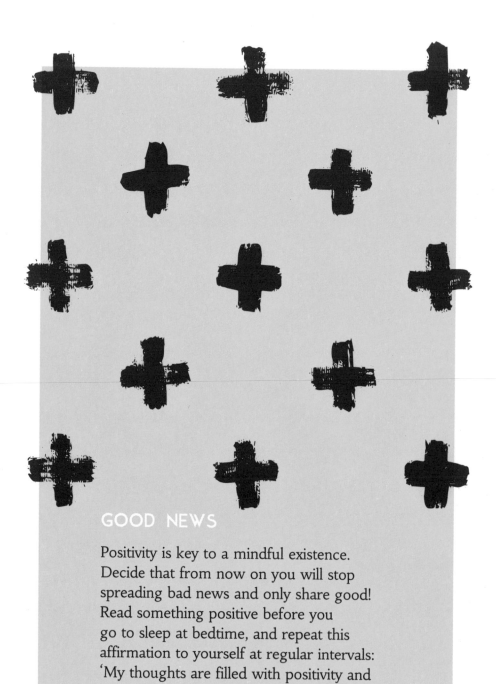

GOOD NEWS

Positivity is key to a mindful existence.
Decide that from now on you will stop
spreading bad news and only share good!
Read something positive before you
go to sleep at bedtime, and repeat this
affirmation to yourself at regular intervals:
'My thoughts are filled with positivity and
my life is brimming with happiness.'

Be happy in the moment, that's enough. Each moment is all we need, not more.

Mother Teresa

PRACTISE ACCEPTANCE

Our natural tendency is to resist painful thoughts or feelings. This means we suffer two 'pains' – the painful situation itself and our resistance to it! For example, you feel stressed because of an impending deadline at work and think, 'I hate feeling so stressed'. The primary pain is stress about your workload. The secondary pain is feeling 'I wish I wasn't so stressed'. The solution is acceptance. Let the unpleasant situation or emotion be as it is, without trying to change it or push it away.

For example, suppose you've just split up with your partner and you are feeling heartbroken. By fighting the pain ('I hate feeling like this, I need this pain to go away') you intensify your suffering. If you accept your feelings, however, you don't heap an extra layer of pain upon the pain you are already feeling – 'I've just broken up with my boyfriend. It's normal to feel sad. It's OK that I feel this way.' Acceptance doesn't mean you like what is happening; it just means you accept that certain things are beyond your control. No matter what the situation, resisting the situation and feelings only magnifies the pain.

CHILDLIKE WONDER

Young children are constantly curious.
They see the magic in everyday things
– a spider, a buttercup or bubbles
in the bath. They teach us to stop
and look again, with amazement, at
what is in front of us. Start viewing
the world through a child's eyes and
see how it brightens up your day!

DO LESS, NOTICE MORE

Instead of cramming as much as possible into your day, do less and do it more slowly, more fully and with more concentration. Take the time to luxuriate in whatever activity you're doing, whether you're cooking supper or chatting to a friend. You should find the experience relaxing and fulfilling when you're not rushing through tasks.

BE THANKFUL

It's easy to get swept away by negative thinking and overlook what is really important. One way to be more positive in your life is to be thankful. People who have a strong sense of gratitude are happier and healthier than those who don't. It's important to take time out to appreciate all the things you usually take for granted. Be thankful for your body and the things it is capable of – hands that let you do so much, legs that take you to so many places, eyes that see the beauty in the world, and heart and lungs constantly working for your survival. This is a far healthier approach than focusing on the body parts you don't like or that are less than perfect in your opinion! Spend a little time each day reflecting on the things you're most grateful for – your health, your loved ones, your dog, the sound of laughter or a beautiful summer's day.

Drink your tea slowly and reverently, as if it is the axis on which the world earth revolves.

Thích Nhât Hạnh

LIGHT A CANDLE

Light a candle and
place it on the table
before you eat. This
brings calm and peace
to a setting, alleviates
tension, and encourages
people to eat more
slowly and thoughtfully.

NAMASTE

The Sanskrit greeting 'namaste' means 'the light in me greets the light in you'. On waking today, decide that you will look for the secret goodness in three people you deal with. Open your heart as you speak with them and notice how this intention affects your thoughts, and the interaction you have with them.

TAKE THREE BREATHS

Whatever your state of mind or the number of things you have to do, rest for a moment between tasks and breathe for at least three complete breaths. This will give you a much needed energy recharge to carry on with your day.

A MINDFUL WORLD

THE SOUND OF WATER

Science has proven that 'blue space' including
seas, rivers and lakes can positively affect
our well-being. The sight, sound, smell and
feel of water calms our frazzled minds and
bodies. For this reason, water is a great aid to
practising mindfulness. The next time you are
in a 'blue space', put your worries to one side
and focus instead on the physical sensations
you are experiencing – the sound of crashing
waves, the smell of salt in the air, the cool
water against your skin or the ripples of a
bubbling stream. This relaxing exercise will
help you to focus on the present moment
and achieve a sense of inner quietness.

YOU ARE NOT ALONE

When you find yourself caught up in a tangle of negative thoughts, place your hand on your heart. See if you can feel it beating and notice how your chest rises and falls with every breath. Think of all the heartbeats doing the same thing across the world, then move on with a renewed sense of shared experience.

SEEK TO EXPAND YOUR

HEART

NOT YOUR POSSESSIONS.

BIRDWATCHING

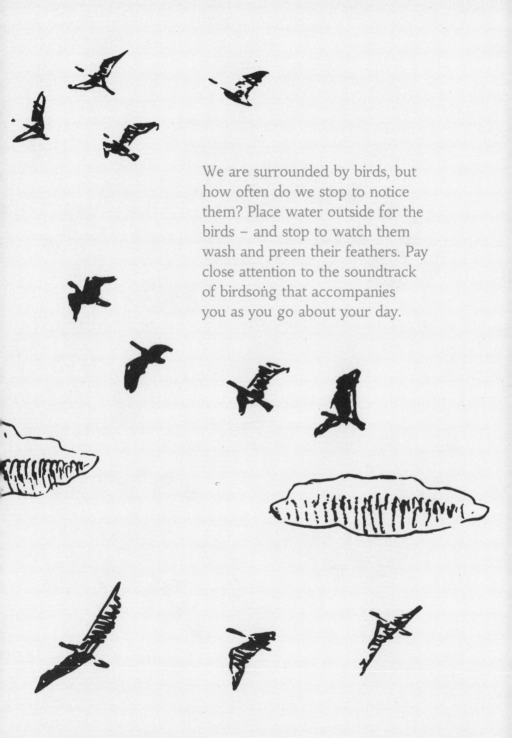

We are surrounded by birds, but how often do we stop to notice them? Place water outside for the birds – and stop to watch them wash and preen their feathers. Pay close attention to the soundtrack of birdsong that accompanies you as you go about your day.

LET NATURE NURTURE YOU

Get up a few minutes early and give yourself time to take a gentle stroll in a quiet, calming space before heading to work. Let your mind wander as you take in the sights and sounds of nature and allow the morning air to revive you.

LOOK AT EVERYTHING AS THOUGH YOU WERE SEEING IT FOR THE FIRST TIME.

When you realise there is
nothing lacking, the whole
world belongs to you.

Lao Tzu

FOCUS ON A FLOWER

Flowers are beautiful objects, but how often do you pause to really drink in their beauty? The next time you're outside, let your gaze settle on a flower. Take in its pure, bright colour and soft, velvety petals, and inhale its delicate fragrance. See its beauty and intricacy, and place all other thoughts to one side while you marvel at the detail of this natural wonder.

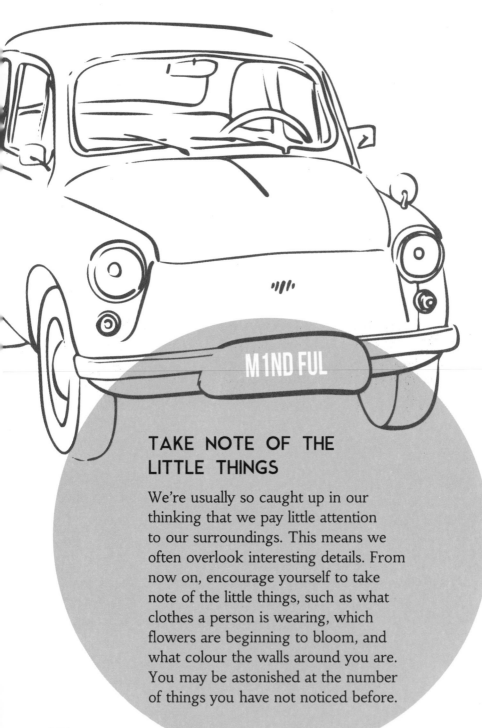

M1ND FUL

TAKE NOTE OF THE LITTLE THINGS

We're usually so caught up in our thinking that we pay little attention to our surroundings. This means we often overlook interesting details. From now on, encourage yourself to take note of the little things, such as what clothes a person is wearing, which flowers are beginning to bloom, and what colour the walls around you are. You may be astonished at the number of things you have not noticed before.

COLOUR THERAPY

Look around you and focus on the colours that you see. Let your eyes wander as you absorb the hues of purple sunsets, yellow pumpkins, ruby berries or the slate-grey sea.

STOP AND SMELL THE ROSES

Tuning into your senses can help you relish the present moment. Enjoy your sense of smell – rain-drenched earth, freshly baked bread, fresh fruit or barbecue smoke. Closing your eyes can sometimes help to heighten your appreciation.

the purpose of life is to enjoy it.

ENCHANTED
FORESTS

Forests and woodlands are ideal places to go back to nature and to feel refreshed. Stand amongst the trees and soak up the peaceful atmosphere. Breathe in the forest smells: the wood's essential oils, moss and soil create magical aromas. Watch beams of light through the leaf canopy, enjoy the textures of rough bark and soft undergrowth, and look out for signs of insects and wildlife. This is something the whole family can relish, if you like – young children can run around, having make-believe adventures and discovering hiding places, while teenagers may be inspired to sit and write poetry or sketch plants and scenery. Don't forget to take a picnic to complete a memorable trip!

THINK LESS FEEL MORE.

REFRESHING RAIN

If you usually avoid
walking in the rain,
don't! A walk in
the rain can bring
another dimension
to your surroundings
and there can be a
heightened sense
of smell, sound and
feeling. As long as you
have a warm place to
dry out afterwards, it
can be refreshing and
revitalising, and can
wash away any blues.

When walking through a bustling city turn your eye to details – chimneys, rooftops, windows and the abundant variety of architectural features. Notice patterns – symmetry, circles, spirals, parallel lines, pairs and repetition. Allow your gaze to stay a moment in wonder as you appreciate the intricacy and beauty of the things humans have created.

THE SOUND OF SILENCE

Make silence a part of your life.
Close your eyes and listen mindfully
for one minute to all the sounds
around you. For one minute, you
have nothing else to do. Just listen.

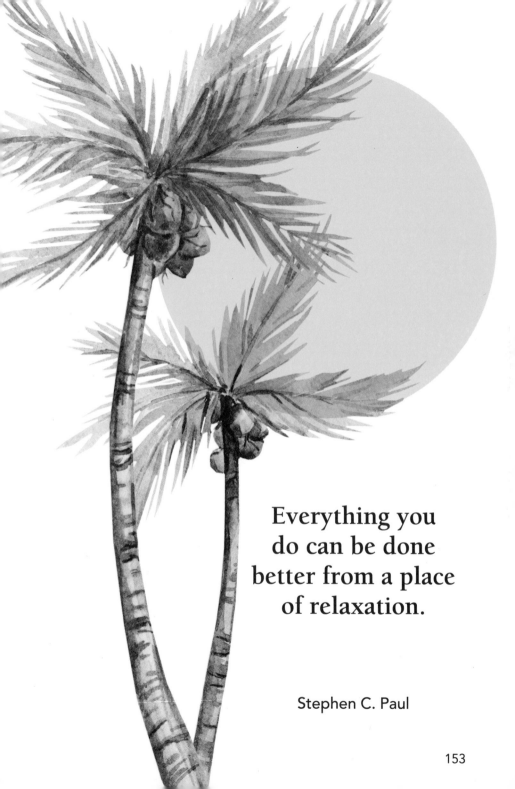

Everything you
do can be done
better from a place
of relaxation.

Stephen C. Paul

You must live in
the present, launch
yourself on every wave,
find your eternity
in each moment.

Henry David Thoreau

GARDEN MEDITATION

If you have your own garden, tune
in to all your senses as you dig the
soil and weed the flowerbeds, or
simply sit and enjoy your lush, green
surroundings. If you don't, visit a public
garden and pay full attention to the
scents, the colours and shapes of your
surroundings, and enjoy their beauty.

MINI MOMENTS OF PEACE

Open up moments of calm throughout your day. This could be a few seconds spent in quiet stillness while the kettle boils or while your computer is switching on, or it could be as simple as taking a deep breath of crisp morning air as you leave the house.

You're only here
for a short visit.
Don't hurry,
don't worry.
And be sure to
smell the flowers
along the way.

Walter Hagen

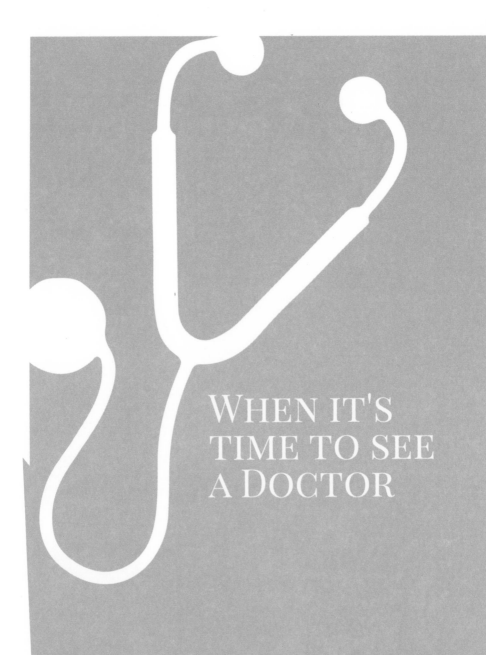

WHEN IT'S TIME TO SEE A DOCTOR

If you've given everything else a try and a worried mind is still proving too much for you, it could be time to seek professional help. Go to your GP first and see what they suggest – they may recommend seeing a therapist, someone you can talk to about your concerns; or cognitive behavioural therapy; or even medication. Remember to be honest with your doctor – try not to hold back, and give as much detail as possible – and they'll be able to suggest the right solution for you and your worries. Complementary therapies can help a great deal to reduce the stresses and strains that could be causing you to feel unbalanced or stressed but sometimes, professional help is what's needed. You'll be on the right track and in safe hands, and will feel the benefit before you know it.

WE HOPE YOU ENJOY THE JOURNEY TOWARDS A NEW, MORE MINDFUL YOU!

Have you enjoyed this book?

If so, why not write a review
on your favourite website?

If you're interested in finding out more about our books,
find us on Facebook at Summersdale Publishers
and follow us on Twitter at @Summersdale.

Thanks very much for buying this Summersdale book.

www.summersdale.com